To. Jago

With Love

from

Mamgu + Grandpa.

Hoping you have lots of fun sorting out the projects in this book!!

CHRISTMAS 2011.

# Contents

# Get Out!

Our mum and dad make films about wildlife, which means we get to see loads of cool animals close up. This book shares some of the things we have discovered about rivers so you can like them as much as we do.

_Fred_

## I'm Fred and I am nine

I really like animals and I like photography. I live right next to a river. It is in the middle of our garden. It is really cool because when you look out of the window you see loads of birds, sometimes kingfishers. There are always lots of colours and it is really nice, especially when the sun is shining or it's just been raining and then the sun shines.

## I'm Gus I am six

frog

I love the river because of the wildlife and it's nice too at night when the moon shines on it. There are a lot of kingfishers and otters on the river. I like to draw the animals I see. Drawing is my favourite thing, and I like to draw maps.

I also like climbing trees and I like going canoeing down the river with Dad and Mum.

Gus

## Our little brother is Arthur

He is three. He can't write yet but he loves to follow us about and try to do what we do, so you will also see him in the book.

He says his favourite creature that lives on the river is a porcupine, but porcupines don't even live here.

Arthur

## Important things to remember

!

When we go exploring on the river we always take Mum and Dad. Rivers can be really dangerous so always take care especially when it's been raining. Wild animals should never be disturbed, you should always try to be quiet and not frighten them. Be especially careful if an animal has babies.

3

# Rivers

Rivers are important to people because they provide:

- irrigation
- rich grazing lands
- transport
- recreation and fun
- habitat for wildlife
- safety

Rivers are really important to humans because of the water they carry.

We can use that water for us and for **animals to drink** and for **watering crops** in the farmers' fields. In very dry parts of the world like parts of **Africa** where there isn't much rain then the **river** is the **main source of water** and the farmers make **irrigation** systems: channels, pipes or ditches that carry water from the river to the plants.

*a river is like a road, sometimes it can be quicker to travel by river*

'Rivers are important for wildlife because lots of animals, like fish, live in them and other animals and us need them for food.' Fred

## Flood Plains

When a river floods then some of the silt, or dirt at the bottom of the river is washed along by the water, this is **really good** for plants to grow in as it is full of **nutrients**.

So the flood plains where a river regularly floods and leaves behind **lots of silt** are good places to grow rich grass which cows and sheep love.

# River Habitats

Different **plants** and **animals** all need different places to **live**, what suits one will not suit another. Adaptations over time mean they **feed, shelter** and **breed** in a particular place.

There is a special word for the particular place that different plants and animals call home; it is **habitat**. There are many different types of habitat  in a river. ⟶

River animals and plants are very interesting because of the **different ways** they live in and around water.

All the animals and plants in this book have special ways of **dealing** with water and the way the **river changes**. You will see that the otter has **webbed feet to swim better**, the dipper has **flaps which seal off its nose** when it goes under the water, and that some of the animals, like the water vole, use the water to help keep them safe. These are called **adaptations.**

It is **up to us** to **look after** all these habitats so that they are **clean,** and **protected,** just right for animals to make their home there. We try to look after the river near us and some of those stories are in this book.

FLOOD meADOW

RiveR BANK

Water

RIVer bEd

5

# Where does water come from?

Water lands as rain and melts from ice in mountains. It flows into streams which become rivers.

Water evaporates from the sea and land to create clouds.

I'm off to the Sargasso Sea

The estuary is where the river ends and the sea begins. An estuary is great wildlife habitat.

Nearly ALL the world's water is stored in the oceans 97%

# Make your own Rain Gauge

Rivers become wider often flooding which creates large flood plains

15
14
13
12
11
10
9
8
7
6
5
4
3
2
1
0

## It is fascinating to see how much rain falls

- Cut the top off a **transparent plastic bottle**.
- Make a **measuring label** on paper by copying the centimetre measurements on your ruler starting with 0.
- Cover it with Sellotape so that it is **waterproof**.
- Stick it to the bottle about a **quarter** of the way up.
- Add a **pebble** and **fill with water** to the 0 mark.
- Turn the cut off top section **upside down** and place inside the bottle to act as a **funnel**.
- Place outside in an open spot and **wait for rain**.

Or you can use an old measuring jug – perfect for the job.

# The river changes

Imagine if this was your home?
**Always different.**
Sometimes there isn't much rain the water can be low and slow.

After lots of rain the river is **high and fast** and sometimes **so noisy** that we have to **shout**. That's why otters, kingfishers and dippers **whistle so loudly.**

Then the kingfisher can only catch **half as many fish** as usual

## In time ...

## Flooding

Sometimes the river floods.
**This affects all the animals** that live on the river bank, and beyond.

This is **Grace** she **lost her mum** after a flood. Their holt must have been filled with water. **We looked after her** till she was fully grown.

## ... and space

The **top** of a river is **narrow, shallow, and fast flowing,** with a **rocky** bottom

# Freezing

In winter the water can turn to ice. The kingfisher can't find any food, and the fish go right to the bottom.

## Pooh sticks world championships

Playing pooh sticks is **great fun** but also shows you **how fast the river flows.**

Next time you play use a stop watch to time the sticks and see just how fast the river flows. After it has rained a lot play in the same place, are the sticks moving faster this time?

We entered the pooh sticks **world championships.** it takes place in Oxfordshire on the river **Thames** in March every year. Anyone can have a go. **Gus nearly won!**

At the **bottom** of the river it is **wider and deeper, slower** with **more silt.** Over time a river can change its path competely.

# Other rivers around the world

Animals that live in rivers all over the world are **often alike**. This is because they have evolved similar ways of finding the **same kind of food** and living on and in the water. So Dad can travel halfway around the world and still film kingfishers and otters but they are **not exactly the same** as the ones here in the UK.

The Amazon is the largest river in the world and flows from the mountains and through the rainforests of South America before heading to the sea. It is home to many wonderful animals.

Our River

Amazon

Zambezi

Anaconda

River dolphin

Caiman

Amazon
South America

Predators
Black caiman will take cubs

1.93m

The giant river otter

## The giant river otter

**Status** Endangered – there are only a few thousand left in the world.

**Facts** Each river otter has a different shaped cream patch on its neck, so it is easy to tell them apart.

Giant river otters live in family groups, this is very unusual for otters.

1.8m

1.3m
The European otter

Food
Piranhas, other fish, snakes, crustaceans

Giant kingfisher
48cm

Pied kingfisher
17cm

European kingfisher
16cm

Malachite kingfisher
13cm

## Kingfisher species

These kingfishers are different colours and sizes, but they all dive into water to catch their food. They all have perching feet for grasping branches, sharp eyesight for spotting fish under the water, and strong beaks for digging nest holes in the river bank. Their bodies are streamlined for speedy diving.

**Giant kingfisher**
Feeds on crabs, fish and frogs. Found in Africa

**Pied kingfisher**
Lives in Africa and Asia

**European kingfisher**
25cm wingspan. Feeds on fish and crayfish.

**Malachite kingfisher**
Feeds on small fish. Found in Africa.

**Guess what**
The average flow rate of water over the falls is the equivalent of 1 million litre bottles of water per second.

This river is most famous for the largest waterfall in the world called the Victoria Falls or Mosi-Oa-Tunya (The Mist that Thunders)

The Zambezi has a variety of animals that are very different from the ones living on our rivers.

Zambezi
Africa

11

# RiVer bEd

The river bed is the **bottom** of the river. River beds can be made from large **rocks**, small **stones**, **gravel**, **sand or silt**. All these kinds of river bed are home to many creatures.

Plants use their roots as anchors.

## Crayfish

Crayfish often live in roots of trees like alder.

## Dipper

Dippers hunt on the river bed

# Stone Loach

'Stone loaches would be scary like monsters if they were big, luckily they're small.' Gus

# Bullhead

Bullheads like to live under stones.

we love exploring the riverbed

# Trout

Trout like to lay their eggs on gravel river beds.

This is Pete he is protecting the white-clawed crayfish

13

# Battle of the crayfish

There are two types of crayfish found in UK rivers, one has always been there, one is new.

## White-clawed crayfish

**Distinguishing features:** Pink to dirty white on the inside of the claws

**Colour:** Green–brown in colour

**Status:** Protected species

**Habitat:** Lives underwater, beneath rocks and in caves, or in tree roots underwater. Nocturnal

**Food:** Scavengers; they eat lots of plant and animal bits but also catch worms and small fish

**Lifespan:** Can live up to 12 years

**Actual size**

'They look like robots when they move.' Gus

The largest type of crayfish is in Tasmania

Scary!

Antenna for feeling for food

**Actual size**

They look like mini monsters but they are **aliens**. Signal crayfish belong in **North America**. People brought them here because they are bigger and better to eat than the native white-clawed crayfish, but then they **escaped** on to our streams.

Strong pincers for capturing food, cutting, attack and defence.

Eyes on moveable stalks

Hard skeleton on the outside – exoskeleton

Tail can be used as a flipper to swim backwards and escape predators

'They pinch with their pincers. They eat. They ambush and they crawl. They look quite like lobsters but not like crabs much.' Gus

'When we found the signal crayfish it was red all over with a tiny white patch on its claw and it is much bigger than the native species. It was like a mini lobster.' Fred

**The *Astacopsis gouldi* may reach 40cm long**

15

# Problems and Conservation

'I don't like the signal crayfish because they spread diseases and we never get to see the white-clawed crayfish.' Fred

## Aliens attack

**Native species** are those that belong here. They have always lived here and have evolved to live in balance with the place where they live. The white-clawed crayfish is the only native species of crayfish in the UK.

**Alien species** upset the balance between native species. Sometimes they take over the places where our native species live or the food that they might eat.

In the UK the signal crayfish is an **alien species.**

## Competition

There is competition between the crayfish species for food. The alien signal crayfish is bigger and better at hunting and so usually wins. This is also called **out competing.**

So when the signal crayfish is around the white-clawed crayfish struggles to get food.

## Diseases
### The crayfish plague

Signal crayfish carry the deadly crayfish **plague**. It doesn't kill them but it kills the white-clawed crayfish. It can travel through a whole river in just days and has **wiped out** most of our native white-clawed crayfish.

# Ark sites

There are no white-clawed crayfish left on our river, or any of the streams that feed into it.

- So that we could film them as part of our river diary, we were taken to a secret location to see the white-clawed crayfish for ourselves. It was very exciting.

- We had to wash our wellies before we got to the stream so that there was no crayfish plague on them.

- We walked a long way up a track to a small stream. It is great habitat for crayfish. It has clear water, lots of rocks and tree roots in the bank.

- All the white-clawed crayfish were gathered from the rivers where they were in danger and put in safer places like this. It is called an Ark Site.

## Crayfish as food

Humans love to eat crayfish, so do otters and kingfishers. They don't seem to mind which type of crayfish they eat.

- Pete, our guide, finally found our first white-clawed crayfish and showed it to us. We took a photo.

- We hope one day that the plague and the signal crayfish will be gone and we can return the white-clawed crayfish to our rivers. Until then they will be safe here.

## Handling crayfish
## Don't do it!

We had permission to pick up the crayfish but don't do it when you are exploring a river, they can **nip**, but also you might spread the **crayfish plague** without knowing it.

'They're mean, when they nipped me, although they were little, it really hurt.' Fred

17

# Dipper

Because we live beside the river the dippers are our neighbours and we see them every day. **They are nosy** and **fun to watch**. They like to sit on the edge of the waterfall.

Every year at the beginning of spring they nest under the bridge and have chicks.

## Why are they called dippers?

**Because they bob up and down**, no one knows why, Fred thinks it is just because they like it.

### Dippers are the only songbird that can swim!

**To go under water they have special adaptations:**

- **eyes** with super focus muscles to see underwater
- **nostrils** that close
- water proof **feathers**
- **blood** that can hold extra oxygen

Our mum can never understand how dippers keep their chests so white...

# 1st Dippers under water

## A world first! –
## An underwater bird table

It's the first time out of the nest.

They love to eat insect larvae or small fish or fish eggs, and even small prawns.

...when they are always in the mud at the bottom of the river.

We wanted to know how dippers swim underwater, so Dad filmed them. He had an underwater camera but needed the dipper to come really close to it, so he put some mealworms in a bowl with some cling film over the top to stop them floating out.

At first the bowl was on a rock above the water, then, when the dipper got used to the food in the bowl, Dad put it under the water. After hours of waiting he got the shot.

When we played it back slowly **we could see how the dipper was swimming.** Like a penguin, it used its wings to stay underwater. It used its beak to turn over stones and stab for food. Its feet could hold on to the rocks. It is the first under-water shot of a wild dipper that we know of!

Dad's special camera

# Bullhead Also called the miller's thumb

**Guess what?** This fish makes a noise! The bullhead can make a knocking sound. It may be to **attract females** or to say **'keep away from my territory'**.

Spines on its back ↓

← 10cm →

Brown with spots

'It looks like someone stamped on its head.' Gus

## Home

### A clean, natural river not too slow-flowing

The river bed, under stones, but not just any old stone.

**Scientists proved that Bullheads love their stone**, when they took away the bullhead's stone and put it further away the bullhead didn't choose a new one but went and found the old one.

## Family

Like sticklebacks the bullhead males look after the babies.

## Defence

### Good camouflage – it is the same colour as the river bed

Kingfishers beware – spines on the back stick in a predator's throat.

## Feeding

### Hunts as night begins to fall (dusk)

Eats, baby fish, insect larvae, crustaceans.

Ambush predator, waits under a stone for prey then swims out quickly to grab them.

Large eyes can see under water in the dark

Large mouth

## Predators

Eaten by brown trout, salmon, pike, heron, kingfisher, dippers and signal crayfish. Otters snack on them, too.

20

# Next-door neighbour is likely to be...
# Stone loach

## Predators
Birds – kingfishers give them to their babies – otters and larger fish like trout.

## Home
**Clear, clean, fast flowing water.**

River bed. Likes sandy or stony bottom. Sometimes buries itself in the sand.

## Feeding
**Nocturnal (at night)**

Swims around using its six feelers or barbels to detect prey on the bottom of the river

Feeds on larvae and crustaceans, such as shrimps like the bullhead, and worms.

*Knock knock*

Barbels or feelers. Four on top lip, two on bottom

## Defence
**Tries to be invisible.**

Very still with brown, yellow and black spots make it hard to see – camouflage

## Alien invader
Signal crayfish are bad news for bullheads. They compete for shelter and food and eat bullhead eggs. Large signal crayfish will even eat adults bullheads.

## Competition
Bullhead, crayfish

8–12cm

Small skinny round body

21

# Breathing underwater

All animals and plants need to breathe, but what about in the river?

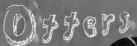

**Humans** need a snorkel to breathe while underwater

**Otters** hold their breath

**Dippers** shut their noses using flaps

Ha Ha!

**Fish** use gills

We can't breathe underwater but plants can.

Gills

TYPHOON
XTS

# Experiment

I wanted to see **how plants breathe underwater.** You can too. **Here's how.**

It doesn't belong in our rivers but **Elodea**, Canadian pondweed, is a great waterweed to experiment with. You can buy it easily from pond or pet shops.

1. Cut off the bottom of a **plastic bottle**, this is your waterweed chamber.

2. Put some Elodea waterweed into it.

3. Turn the chamber **upside down** in a larger jar of water and make sure that there are **no air spaces**.

4. Place in a dark cupboard.

5. In the morning, you can see proof that the waterweed has been **breathing**. There is a **bubble** making the chamber float.

**Elodea**

**6.** The gas in the bubble is carbon dioxide.

23

# Catching tiddlers

## The best way to spend an afternoon

## What to take

- ✔ **An old sieve** for sorting small creatures from silt
- ✔ **Jam jars**
- ✔ **Magnifying glass**
- ✔ **Nets**
- ✔ **Ice cream tub** for looking at things in
- ✔ **Field guide** for looking things up
- ✔ **Camera** with a macro lens, even the basic ones have one (Gus has a waterproof camera its great)
- ✔ **Note pad** and paper
- ✔ **Spare socks and clothes** (we always get wet)
- ✔ **Snacks and drinks** (we always get hungry)

## What should you do?

**Move slowly** so that you don't kick up a huge amount of mud and the water stays clear.

Pretend you are a dipper, **lift stones** and hold your net or jar in the water flow to catch creatures.

**Look underneath** the stone, what is gripping on to it?

If you were an otter you would search for fish in the water. Use your net near the bank under overhanging plants, or under stones looking for a tasty otter snack like a bullhead.

Just investigate everywhere...

Don't Splash!

## What might you find?

**Fish**
- ☐ Minnows
- ☐ Sticklebacks
- ☐ Bullheads
- ☐ Stone Loaches

**Insects**
- ☐ Mayfly nymph
- ☐ Caddis fly larvae
- ☐ Dragonfly larvae
- ☐ Water scorpion

**Snails**

**Freshwater shrimp** – see how it swims backwards, it is small enough to hide between stones

Go dipping at the same place at different times of year, you will find different things.

After you have inspected photographed and recorded your creatures you must **let them go.**

## What do you have to remember?

If you find a safe shallow rocky place on a good day when the water is slow river dipping is great fun. **BUT** always take a grown-up and stay with them. Look at the river before you paddle, and ask questions:

- has it been raining?
- is the river flowing too fast?
- could it knock you over?
- is it too deep or below your wellies?
- what is the bottom like? If it is soft mud you might sink in it.

Use a long stick to test the bottom if you can't see it.

Stickleback

Caddis fly larva

New discoveries

Minnow

Tadpoles

25

# Water

The water is what makes the river special. It is **always moving** sometimes **fast** sometimes **slowly**.

Trout

Gulp! will my spines protect me

sticklebacks

dragonfly

Mmmmm tasty stickleback

Cripes what a lot of predators

water beetle

If **chemicals** get into the water then it can become **dirty or polluted**. Animals and plants need **clean water** to live in.

Oh good stickleback for tea

otter

Eels

# Dragonflies

Dragonflies are winged insects
of the river and wetlands

Larva

**Larva climbs stem**

**Old skin splits**

**Humans go:** baby → **child** → grown up

**Insects go:** egg → **larva or nymph** → grown up

Metamorphosis – For some insects like dragonflies
the grown up body is completely different.
(Larva is one, larvae is more)

'I don't like it when they catch things
they make me jump.' Gus

'They look quite weird.
They eat baby sticklebacks,
which I like.' Gus

## Dragonfly nymph or larva

Live underwater for up to **5 years**

They are **ambush** predators they hunt for prey
using big eyes and **jaws** that suddenly pop out to
stab and grab.

'They are very ugly and very
formidable in mini world although
not formidable to us.' Fred

'They are really unusual and don't remind
me of anything else. I saw one swim all
the way up to the top of the water and he
swam all the way up and caught a fish and
started to eat it.' Fred

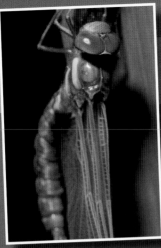

New dragonfly comes out. It is soft

Its wings unfold, pump up and go hard

Adult

No lessons required – somehow the dragonfly already knows how to fly

Six Pairs of jointed legs

They have a hard outer skeleton

# Dragonflies

- **Patrol their territory** around ponds or rivers or streams

- Are very **beautiful**

- In the UK there are about **30 different types** – like the common darter

- Dragonflies have been around for **300 million years** – that's before the dinosaurs

## New discovery

When Dad filmed dragonflies with a **super slow motion** camera he discovered that their wings beat **55 times per second**

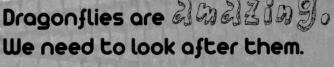

**Dragonflies are amazing. We need to look after them.**

- Look after wetlands, **Don't pollute** the water.
- **Dig a pond.** Our wildlife pond is a new home to lots of dragonflies.
- Join the **British Dragonfly Society.**

29

# Mayfly

Mayfly are insects. We have the same body all our lives but many insects, like the mayfly, change body forms.

The eggs in the water grow and start the life cycle again.

Mayfly spend the first two years of their life as a nymph underwater.

There are **46** different **species** of mayfly found in **Britain**.

The female lays her eggs on the surface of the water.

The male and female die at the end of the day; most land on the river, some get eaten.

Then the mayfly changes.

The mayfly have a special dance. They fly straight up and fall down in the air many times it is called spinning.

The male and female mate.

Dad filming the mayfly hatch

'Sometimes they look like fairies flying away.' Gus

# A mayfly feast

Once a year for just a few weeks all the mayfly hatch out of the river. Sometimes there are lots all hatching at the same time. **Look for mayfly on your local river** in the last two weeks of May and the first week of June as they emerge out of the water.

The mayfly hatch is a **feast** for lots of animals. Birds are working really hard to feed their babies at this time of year so the mayfly, which are easy to catch, are a **tasty treat**.

Spend some time sitting and watching the river. **Count** how many creatures you see feasting on mayfly.

Try to spot river birds like **ducks** and **moorhens** but also look out for other birds like **robins** or **thrushes**. **Trout** also like mayfly, if you can wait long enough and watch the water carefully, you might see one **leap out** of the water to catch them.

Yum!

The mayfly hatch is a beautiful part of river life.

I'm hungry

# Sticklebacks

Sticklebacks have three spines on their backs!

Britain's smallest freshwater fish
Life size 10cm long!

## Our Frank

- In the tank we could watch a stickleback bring up his family. The dads do all the work the mums lay the eggs and go.

- First Frank built a nest in a hole in a log.

- Then he got a female to lay eggs in it.

- He looked after the eggs fanning water on them.

- When the eggs hatched he had to protect the babies. There were hundreds of them. All the minnows and dragonfly larvae were trying to eat them.

Minnows on the hunt for food

We built a tank in the garden to film underwater life.

# Predators

**Kingfishers like to eat sticklebacks**

Trout, perch, pike and herons also like to eat sticklebacks

'It was like *Star Wars* but we called it fish wars.' Gus

# Guess what
sticklebacks are related to seahorses

Phew!

'They are usually brown but in spring and summer the males get blue eyes and red bellies to attract females when they want to have babies.' Fred

Dragonfly larvae prey on the baby sticklebacks

# THE MYSTERIOUS EEL MIGRATION

Sometimes eels can go over land, a thick skin and slime stops them drying out.

## migration

**Of the incredible journeys that some animals make the eel migration is full of mystery.**

### 2. Gulf Stream

They drift as larvae on a current called the **Gulf Stream** to Europe.

### 4. Return

### 1. Sargasso Sea

■ No one knows where eels are born, all we know that it is somewhere in the **Sargasso Sea** south of Bermuda.

■ Many years later, in the autumn on a **moonless cloudy night** when the river is full they begin to travel again. They make a **6,000km** journey back to the **mystery location** in the Sargasso Sea to lay eggs and die. The eels never return.

### 3. Freshwater development

■ In winter and spring they get to Europe. They move up rivers as tiny 'see through' eels called **glass eels**.

■ They become **elvers**. They now have colour and grow quickly. They **hunt at night** feeding on snails and insect larvae, frogs, small fish and crayfish.

■ They grow into **yellow eels**.

■ Next they become adult and change to **silver eels**.

### Another mystery

Eels don't have sat-nav. So how do they find their way around the world?

'The eel was really slimy. Dad told me off for wiping eel slime on my trousers, but I didn't want it on my hands.' Gus

# Conservation

The eel is **critically endangered** – that means it might be **extinct** soon.

Eels are slimy snake-like fish – otters love eating them.

Eels are important food for river animals. Birds, otters and herons love them.

'When we found an eel in our river we were really surprised because Dad thought there weren't any left.' Fred

Weirs block the eels' migration

We can't see under the water so how do we know what fish are there or if there are enough for kingfishers and otters to live on?

# Electrofishing

## by Fred

allows us to safely stun the fish so that we can count them.

Rubber suits prevent electrocution

Control box

Generator ~ creates electricity

Fish tank.

UH OH!

~ Electrical current

The water conducts electricity

## Environment Agency

The environment agency is responsible for caring for our environment in the UK and especially our rivers.

'Their work is helpful to the animals because they can check how healthy the animals are and they are pretty important because without them there would be litter and pollution in a lot of rivers. Then all the fish and plants would die without clean water and the ducks and otters and mink would die because there would be no food.' Fred

Electrofishing was cool. They had **long poles like light sabres** with round metal wires on the end of them. They plugged the wire into the machine and the machine produced electricity, which electrocuted the fish but they didn't die, which was good because I didn't want them to die. The electricity can flow through the water.

When I first saw them floating on the surface of the river it was different from what I had imagined because I thought they would sink. I thought they were dead until someone told me that they were only stunned.

We had to catch the fish and lie them down on a board with centimetres on it and then we measured them quickly so that they wouldn't run out of breath. It was a bit difficult because they kept jumping about trying to escape and they were very slimy.

We found **the biggest trout we've ever seen** on our river he was 42cm and we found dace which I hadn't seen before. If we have a big fish then we have a healthy river because it means there is lots of food for them and clean water to live in and lots of free space to swim in.

Dace

But my favourite thing that we did that day was **putting the fish back in the river.**

# Discoveries

When you discover something always take time to ask questions.

## What did you expect to happen?

I thought we would find more fish, there were fewer than I expected but lots of types.

## Why do you think that was?

In different places we found quite different fish, although that is quite weird because the water temperature didn't change or anything so maybe it was because there was more sun where there were no trees, or maybe it was to do with hiding from predators. In some places it is deep and in some it is shallow some fish prefer the deep water and some fish don't.

# RIVER BANK

The river banks are on the edge of the river. They offer **great homes** to lots of **different creatures**, which use the bank in different ways.

The kingfisher digs **tunnels** in a muddy bank to **nest in**.

*Kingfisher*

The kingfisher uses its beak to dig a nest

*water vole*

Himalayan Balsam

water Shrew

'Water shrews are very secretive. Mum saw one but we have never seen one. They venomous teeth.' Fred

Otter

Flag iris

Water vole colonies are **like towns** they have runs, latrines and tunnels in **the bank** to live in.

The otter sleeps near the bank in a holt, like this hollow space under a willow tree.

Moorhens and ducks build nests on the river bank in spring.

Poo

Ducks and Moorhens

# The true story of the water vole

### (Arvicola terrestris)

ONCE UPON A TIME, in a small ditch, lived a water vole called Harvey Cola. Harvey was dark brown and furry and about 12cm long with a nice furry tail. He lived with his family in the ditch. He had lots of brothers and sisters because his mum had two sets of babies every summer; sometimes she had five at a time, so Harvey was always surrounded by other water voles!

Their ditch was as perfect as a place could be for voles: the water was clean and, because the banks were so sunny, there was plenty to eat. Harvey could swim and play and life was good.

Harvey didn't know it, but he was very famous. People all over the world loved to read about a water vole just like him. That vole was called Ratty and he was a character in a book called *The Wind in the Willows* by Kenneth Grahame. Even though it was over 100 years old this book was still very popular.

Harvey didn't know much about people at all, just that they often came walking past his ditch with their sniffy dogs. Sometimes when he was munching on some grass or nuts they would hear people coming and dive to safety in the water leaving just a 'plop' sound. Under the water, Harvey and his brothers and sisters swam to their burrow entrance, a small underwater hole. Once inside it was dry and they were warm and safe because no predator could follow them.

If they needed to go to the toilet they had an outside toilet called a latrine; it was easy to find because the side of the ditch had runways like vole roads running down it. If you didn't know where to go you just followed the runway. Mum said that vole latrines were important because if other voles saw your outside toilet they would not try to move in. Mum also said that the ditch used to be very busy with voles living all the way up it and into the river beyond. Now, she said there were not as many voles as there used to be.

One day, when Harvey went to use the toilet he had to stop dead on the run. There standing in the ditch was a person, a woman with

long hair dangling. She was pointing at their outside toilet and saying, **'Look a latrine! I've found the poo.'**

Harvey was so frightened he couldn't move. He just sat under the cover of some nettles and watched. A man with fur on his face walked up the ditch, he was holding some leftovers that Harvey and his brother and sisters hadn't eaten that morning.

**'Look!'** he said holding up the stalks of tough grass. **'A classic sign. See how these have been chewed at an angle.'**

**'This is fantastic!'** said the lady. She picked up an old piece of Harvey's poo and rubbed it between her fingers. **'See it is green with round edges. This is definitely water vole poo.'**

Harvey thought this was very odd. He knew that he was safely hidden and decided to keep very still.

Then he realised that there were three small people on the side of the ditch, peering at the poo and at the leftovers.

**'Look boys, we've got water voles,'** said the lady.

**'But they're endangered aren't they?'** said the boy with white fur.

**'Yes they are very precious.'**

Harvey pricked his tiny ears, this lady must know what she is talking about.

**'They are the fastest declining mammal in the UK.'**

**'What's a mammal?'** said the middle small person with brown fur.

**'Any warm-blooded animal with a backbone, just like us.'**

Harvey was just thinking that he looked nothing like them when he began to feel uncomfortable, like he wanted to run fast or dive in the water, he realised that he had been seen.

The smallest person, who was really very small with thick glossy brown fur on top of his head and twinkly eyes, was smiling down at him.

**'Water vole,'** he said.

# Plop!

# The menacing mink

A few days later Harvey's mum was having babies again so he and his brothers were playing dare. Lately they had been finding apples in the end of the ditch just past the outdoor toilet.

Apples didn't normally end up in the ditch and they were sweet and delicious, but next to them was always sitting a strange, hard animal with one black, round shiny eye. It made noises but didn't move; it wasn't like any animal they had seen before and Harvey didn't really like it. Now that he was the biggest and strongest brother it was down to Harvey to dash down the ditch, grab the apple with his strong front teeth and drag it backwards.

**'Three, two, one, go!'** Harvey scampered through the mud, straight to the apple. As his teeth sank into it he heard the strange animal next to him start whirring. Heave! He pulled the apple back,

heave, and further back until he was just out of view. But then, freeze! Another sound that Harvey knew. It was the smallest small person again and he was talking about water voles. Ahead in the ditch a pair of giant legs appeared.

Harvey kept still behind the apple. It smelt so sweet and juicy, he longed to crunch into it. The giant person reached down to the still creature and grabbed it.

**'We've got it, we've got a shot!'**

**'Lets have a look.'**

Harvey could see them all sitting down, peering at the strange animal.

**'Ohhhhh look,'**

**'A water vole. Look he's stealing the apple.'**

Harvey peered out; how did they know? They couldn't see him, he just didn't understand that they were looking at a camera. The people stood up to go. The smallest person stared into the ditch.

**'What are we going to do about the mink though?'**

**'One visit from the mink will wipe them all out. He is small enough to get in through the underwater entrance – he'll eat them all in a night.'**

**'It's worrying that we found mink footprints so close.'**

**'Bye water vole,'** said the smallest small person looking right at Harvey.

The voices faded.

Harvey was really worried now. A new predator that could swim underwater and was small enough to fit into their burrow and that would eat them. No wonder they were in danger.

WATER VOLE

MINK

That night none of them could rest. There were strange smells in the ditch. Harvey went to use the latrine and found new footprints, star-shaped ones that he hadn't seen before. 'The new predator' he thought. 'We haven't time to work out how to escape from a new predator.'

But then on the air came another smell he knew very well. It was still only faint – but he knew what it meant – an otter was coming.

Back in the burrow he normally felt safe, but now he was not sure. There were strange noises in the ditch.

Suddenly, a large dark grey head appeared from the underwater entrance. Too small to be an otter, it looked more like a weasel, but a weasel can't swim underwater – this must be the mink.

**'We are all doomed!'** squealed his mother, holding her babies tight, and bravely baring her long teeth. And indeed it seemed as though they were.

But suddenly from outside came a high pitched whistle, then another – two otters were calling each other. The mink froze, hearing the sound. Two otters were a frightening prospect, he didn't want to get caught by them hunting in their patch. He looked back at Harvey's family, he was tempted to eat them as he had eaten every other water vole on the river, but it was too risky to hang about. The mink disappeared.

Harvey could breathe again, the water vole family were safe, and because the otters stayed on the river the mink never returned.

For a long time there were no otters on our rivers because there was too much pollution, but now they are coming back. They are more powerful hunters than mink and in competition with them seem to win. So we hope that water vole families all over the country are safe and that they can breed and start to live up and down all our rivers, just like they always have.

Of course we will have to play our part too; we should keep our eye on the mink and make sure our rivers are clean.

## The End

otter

# OTTERS

**A strong tail**
for swimming fast

*body wiggles to swim*

**Super thick fur**

stops body heat being
lost to water. Two layers:

- **waterproof** layer
  on top like a coat
- warm **thermal layer**
  underneath like
  a fleece

**Sharp teeth**
for holding and
eating prey

**Webbed feet**
push through water

**Nostrils**

**on the top of the nose**
allow the otter to breath
while in the water

Closed when under-
water

*open*

**Ears**
can close under water

*open*

*closed*

*closed*

**Eyes**
can see underwater –
without goggles!

# Sometimes new discoveries are right under our noses!

## While we were filming we discovered something new...

'We thought otters could **smell under water** and we wanted to **prove it**. We got a trout from the fishmonger and tied it to a brick at the bottom of a river. We put an **underwater camera** next to it with wires trailing back to the kitchen, so we could **watch** what **happened** to the trout.

Suddenly the water went brown and the otter was there, it took the trout! When we watched it back we could see that it **sniffed the trout;** a bubble came **out of its nose** and went **back in.**

I was so excited because I think we had just **discovered something new** about otters.'

Dad keeps a close eye on the action

# otter tracking

Otters are **always on the move**, they have **large territories** and visit the **same places**. They are really **hard to see** so look for otter signs as often as you can.

## Tracks

Look for **tracks in wet mud** or sand beside a river. **Count the toes** – an otter, a mink and a badger **have five**, a dog and fox only have four.

### It is fun to make a mould.

1. Find a good footprint.

2. Cut out a ring from a plastic drinks bottle.

3. Carefully place the ring around the print.

4. Use the bottom of the bottle as a bowl to mix up plaster o Paris with water, it needs to be thick but still runny. Be careful to follow the instructions on the plaster of Paris, it does really heat up and can burn skin.

Leaving a smelly poo is a way of saying ...

"This is my place"

"I am here"

## Spraint = POO!

Look for spraint on rocks like this one, which sticks out of the water.

The otters on our river leave spraint on some willow roots, which stick out from the side of the bank, and we usually find them at the end of the waterfall where the otter climbs out of the river on to the bank.

Use a stick to poke the spraint and see what the otter has been eating. Can you see fish bones or scales or even crayfish parts?

Does it really smell? Otter poo actually smells nice – sweet and fishy.

Most other animals have nasty smelling poo.

5. Pour it into the ring all over the footprint.

6. Wait around 30 minutes until it is cold and hard.

7. Remove cast and brush off any clinging dirt.

5.

6.

Of course you can do this with any kind of footprint not just otter.

## Why not make a collection?
Don't forget to include your own.

'When you see an otter it is awesome, that's why they are my favourite animal, and because Dad films them. They are cute. While you are waiting to see them you might get cold and bored, but if you haven't seen one you would really like to.' Fred

# Otter watching
If you plan to go otter watching you will have to be **still and quiet** for a long time. Take a grown-up as the best time is **just as darkness falls**.

■ Remember **warm clothes** and pack something to eat and drink.

■ On the river bank **listen for high whistles**, which mean that a mum and cubs are on their way.

■ If you see an otter **remember** do not disturb it. Otters are the **ultimate stealth animal**, if you are too noisy you won't see one.

Seeing an otter is really hard in the wild and you can't normally see them underwater, but if you do, it's amazing.

# Kingfishers

Kingfishers have their own patch or territory on the river – they will fight other kingfishers who come to fish there.

## Dive masters

**Super fast** dive means fish can't escape.

Eyes that can **see through** reflections into the water.

Favourite prey are bullheads and minnows.

They can catch **55 to 60** fish a day when they are feeding babies.

'I do like the blue because blue is my favourite colour. But I don't like it when they just sit in one place staring because that is boring.' Gus

You can tell which are the female kingfishers, they have an **orange** bottom beak.

'The kingfisher is Dad's favourite he has been watching them since he was nine.' Fred

# Tyndall effect

The sky is **not blue**, nor is a kingfisher.

Kingfisher feathers are special – blue light **doesn't bounce back** from them but all other colours do, this makes them look like they are blue. This is called the Tyndall Effect.

The kingfisher looks like a jewel but it is really **just brown.**

'I like watching them because they will get really close to you if you are really quiet and still.' Fred

'I like kingfishers because they are very colourful and very fast and I like fast animals. When they go past they look like a streak of blue.' Fred

# How to spot a kingfisher

- The most important thing is to **stay still**, so make sure you have warm clothes on.

- Look for kingfishers in **town and country**. We have seen them on the Thames in the middle of Chiswick.

- Look for a likely fishing perch, it might have white kingfisher poo around it.

- **Try to blend in.** In the city sit quietly, in the country hide behind a branch or bush.

- You might have to wait for **up to an hour** or just a few minutes if you are very lucky.

- Listen out for a blast of **high-pitched whistles** which says the kingfisher is coming.

- Look out for a streak of blue. **If you are lucky** the kingfisher will land on the perch near you and fish from it.

- **KEEP STILL!** And you might see lots of other animals too!

**Each dive takes less than 2 seconds**

# Plant survival techniques

## Golden flag iris

### A native species

### Stem
Tall stem 1.5m, taller than most of our other flowers. Leaves are sword shaped.

### Growth
The same plant grows back again every year.

## Roots: tubers (survival booster)

The golden flag iris grows from tubers, like hard sponges, they have air tunnels in them so that they can still hold oxygen even when they are underwater.

This means that they can survive in the mud where the water meets the bank, a place which is often underwater and where other plants struggle.

The tuber acts as a food store all through the winter when the rest of the plant dies down.

### Flower
Invisible marks that only insects can see act like lights on a airport runway to guide the flying insects to the right landing place to find the nectar.

Watch out for demoiselles and dragonflies

The golden flag iris near our house is a great home for the beautiful demoiselles; they perch on the stems and lay their eggs in the stream.

# Himalayan balsam

## The alien invader

Grows on the river bank and stony areas on the side of the river called shoals.

Because of its beauty it was brought from other countries to grow in people's gardens but then it escaped from the gardens to the rivers and …

### …created problems.

## Flower

Bees prefer it, because it has more sweet nectar than native flowers. So they pollinate it first.

## Seeds (survival booster)

Each plant can produce **800 seeds**, that's a lot! They shoot out from exploding seed pods and land up to SEVEN metres away. If they land in the water the seeds can be transported down the river, to take over somewhere new.

7 metres

## Stem

1 to 2 metres high, this plant grows really tall (taller than our dad who is 6 foot 4, and three times the size of Gus). Himalayan Balsam grows faster and higher than other wildflowers and grows well any where. **It steals the other wildflowers fair share of sunlight.**

'I like it when we pulled it out because it was easy for me.' Gus

## Get out: Balsam bashing

Help our wildflowers – get out in June before the balsam flowers and makes seeds, and just pull it up, remember its weakness is those small roots; even though they are huge plants they are easy to pull up …

## Roots

The roots do not grow very deep and hold on to rocks and soil.

51

# Mallard ducks and moorhens

They are common in both town and country.

## Nesting

Ducks have to sit on their eggs to keep them warm for 28 days and protect them. If they choose a place that is not safe they might lose their eggs.

## Food

Water insects, seeds and plants from the water. Feeds in the fields too, likes grain.

'It is funny to watch the ducklings learn to jump off the waterfall. You'd think they would be hurt but they are fine.' Fred

## Chicks

Ducklings are small and they get hunted at night. Dad filmed an otter hunting them in the dark, their mum had to be really brave to protect them.

'One year a noise woke us in the night. In the torchlight we could see a badger eating all the eggs out of the duck's nest.' Gus

Mallard ducks

# Moorhen

**Green legs**

## Food

Insects, seeds, plants, snails.

## Chicks

The moorhens had six ugly babies this year but they were still really cute.

Dark brown body which looks black

Red bill with yellow tip (a white bill means it is a coot)

## Nesting

Usually likes to make a nest in reeds on the bank but while we were filming they nested at the top of a tree. The moorhen lives on the bank but feeds in the water and fields too.

# WANTED!
## for raiding nests for eggs

Otter

Mink

Rat

53

# FLood meADow

Bush vetch – can climb to the sunshine by clinging on to tall grasses.

**Are plants boring? Nooooooo. The flowers are so cool. If you don't believe us get your camera and get really close!**

Also all the insects moths and butterflies will die without them and in the end so would we. They are REALLY important.

Flood meadows are rare, their plants are special because they don't mind having their roots in water sometimes but that means they don't really live anywhere else. We need to look after these unusual places.

Yorkshire fog

Meadow buttercup

Moths

54

Some moths have colours that help camouflage them.

Bees

To get the biggest number of different flowering plants we must mow the meadow twice a year and clear it. That gives room for more plants to grow ... and Arthur loves mowing!

'In the spring the meadow is yellow with meadow buttercups. In the summer it changes as different plants produce flowers.' Fred

Bee orchid is a rare find here, can you see it mimics a bee?

Cowslip

'It's a sort of bee because its got that bee flower because bees will marry a flower and then the flower goes nowhere and the bees fly off and then the flower dies and then the bees die.' Gus

# Bees

Yes **bees can sting** but they are **very precious** because of:

## Pollination

**Bee visits flower**

**Collects nectar to turn into honey**

**At the same time pollen rubs off onto the bee**

**Flower can now make seeds and new plants can grow**

**Bee visits next flower**

**Pollen rubs off in next flower and fertilisation occurs**

56

Plants up and down the river bank and all around the **flood meadow**, from tiny flowers to big trees, all need **pollination** to make new plants.

Although we love them, flowers are only beautiful and smell nice to attract the bees and other insects.

Other insects and birds and even the wind can help spread pollen but **bees are really good.**

*Guess what?*
Different types of bee have different length tongues for different types of flowers!

**Pretend** your little finger is a bee and gently push it into a flower, **can you see** the pollen, like **dust** on your finger?

**The alien invader**

Bees like Himalayan balsam best – it has the most nectar.

So **thanks to the bees** we have a flood meadow full of **flowers** and also lots of **honey!**

# Amazing Moths

## Fantastic facts

There are over **2500** different kinds of moth in the UK.

Moths usually fly at night but **some can fly in the day**.

Moths can be just **as brightly coloured as butterflies** but some have dull colours for camouflage.

Moths **feed on sweet nectar** which they find in flowers.

Moths are an important source of food for many birds, bats and mammals.

Some moths have good hearing which helps them detect bat predators and avoid them.

The elephant hawk moth is often found around rivers and streams.

Some moths are hairy which helps them **stay warm**.

## Moth habitats

Moths like rivers because there are so many different flowering plants up and down the river banks where they can find food. But **moths live everywhere** in cities and countryside.

The Atlas moth is the largest moth in the world.

Moths have amazing names.
There are:

- Dark-barred twin-spot carpet
- Beautiful carpet
- Bleached pug
- Drinker
- Hoary footman
- Ruby tiger
- Peppered
- Elephant hawk
- Buff ermine

It lives in Southeast Asia and can have massive a 30cm wing span.

30cm

## Making a difference

Not much is known about moths so if you study and record what you find, one day you could make a big difference, like finding a rare species.

# Moth trapping

In the holidays when you don't have to get up early for school, why not have a moth sleepover with your friends like we did and try some of these things out. You can trap in any season and even in the town. Take care, though, the most important thing is to let the moths go free again unharmed.

'I really liked moth trapping because my best friend Thomas was there and because they are really interesting and colourful not just brown things like everyone thinks they are.' Fred

## Traps and trapping

Moths are attracted to light – this makes them easy to catch.

■ Choose a night with little rain and no wind – warm cloudy and calm is the best weather for moth trapping.

■ Set up the trap at dusk with a grown-up. Choose a place that won't get too hot when the sun rises.

■ Place old egg trays or boxes in the bottom. Moths like to crawl under them and hide.

■ Remember different moths like different places so try trapping in different habitats. We put one by the pond, one in the meadow and one by the river.

■ In the morning check your moth traps as early as you can. Moth wings are precious and fragile, take care not to touch them.

■ Don't forget to write down what you see and if you have a camera take lots of photos to help you remember the details of the moths later.

■ Identify your moths.

■ Let all the moths go.

## Rainy day activity

Use an old cardboard box as a pretend moth trap and make the moths to go in it. Draw them then cut them out of tracing paper, greaseproof paper, newspaper, old magazines or plain paper.

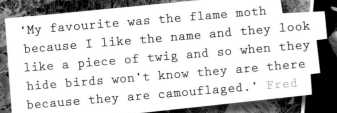

## Make your own nectar

You and your adult helper will need:

**500ml cola**
**1kg dark brown sugar**
**1 tin black treacle**
**an old paint brush**
**an old container**
**a torch**

Into a pan pour, 500ml cola, 1kg dark brown sugar, 1 tin black treacle. Heat and stir until all the ingredients are dissolved, allow to bubble gently for two minutes. Get an adult to pour the mixture into a small bucket or old Tupperware container. (Take extra care the mixture is really hot and will stick to your skin if you spill it).

## Other ways to find moths

After dark shine a bright torch at a white sheet and wait for moths to come, even a low energy light bulb in a porch or shed will do the trick.

Or just try searching flowering plants with a torch for an hour or two after dusk.

What will you find? Use the butterfly conservation website (at the back of this book) or a good wildlife book to help you identify your moths.

Amazingly **we found 55 different species,** before we tried moth trapping we had no idea they were even there!

▮ Elephant hawk moth caterpillars have a long snout like a trunk.

▮ You can find them in May, June, July and August in England and Wales.

▮ They have brilliant night vision; they can even see different colours at night.

61

# Get connected!

www.butterflyconservation.org
This is really useful for help with identification of butterflies and moths, look out for the moths count pages.

www.arkive.org
Discover the world of wildlife with photos, films and games.

www.wildlifewatch.org.uk
Run by the wildlife trusts for wildlife explorers.

www.wwt.org.uk
Find out where your nearest centre is and go and discover wetlands for yourself.

www.rspb.org.uk/youth
A section of the Royal Society for Protection of Birds good for having fun and finding facts.

www.dragonflysoc.org.uk
Home of the British dragonfly society.

www.plantlife.org.uk
A charity devoted to protecting and helping the conservation of wild plants.

www.halcyonmedia.org
Our own website, with a link to Charlie's website for great wildlife photos.

**Get Out and explore your local river**
Philippa Forrester and Fred, Gus and Arthur Hamilton James

preface

Published by Preface 2010

Copyright © Philippa Forrester 2010

Philippa Forrester has asserted her right to be identified as the author of this work under the Copyright, Designs and Patents Act 1988

First published in Great Britain in 2010 by
Preface Publishing
20 Vauxhall Bridge Road
London SW1V 2SA

An imprint of The Random House Group Limited
**www.rbooks.co.uk**
**www.prefacepublishing.co.uk**

Addresses for companies within The Random House Group Limited can be found at www.randomhouse.co.uk

The Random House Group Limited Reg. No. 954009

A CIP catalogue record for this book is available from the British Library

ISBN 978 1 84809 226 6

Design: Nick Heal and Craig Stevens
Illustration: Jake Biggin

Printed and bound by GGP Media, Pössneck, Germany

## Photography

© **Mark Carwardine**: river dolphin, page 10; © **iStockphoto.com/ Eric Isselèe**: porcupine, page 3; © **iStockphoto.com/Valeriy Evlakhov**: boat, page 4; © **iStockphoto.com/George Clerk**: piranha, page 10; © **iStockphoto.com/Torsten Karock**: caiman, page 10; © **iStockphoto.com/Johnny Lye**: river Amazon, page 10; © **iStockphoto.com/Daniel Schumaher**: anaconda, page 10; © **iStockphoto.com/Yan Gluzberg**: nesting duck, page 52; © **iStockphoto.com/Chris Crafter**: badger, page 52; © **iStockphoto. com/Val Thoermer**: rat, page 53; © **iStockphoto.com/Floris Slooff**: Atlas Moth, page 58; © **Tom Patterson**: map, page 34; © **Vectorportal.com**: flags, pages 14, 15. **All other photos are copyright of the authors** with contributions from **Nick Heal, Ian Llewellyn** and **Richard Taylor-Jones.**

# Spotting and fact cards

Kingfisher

Otter

Duck

Eel

Dragonfly

Stickleback

Bullhead

Crayfish

Get extra points. If you spot the animal you earn the spotability points.

## Eel — 80

| Adapting Powers | 25 |
|---|---|
| Shape, life-cycle, gills | |
| Predator | 20 |
| Prey | -20 |
| Survivability | 15 |
| Threatened species | |
| Spotability | 40 |
| Difficult to spot in wild | |

SPOTTED

## Duck — 55

| Adapting Powers | 25 |
|---|---|
| webbed feet, waterproof | |
| Predator | 5 |
| Prey | -10 |
| Survivability | 25 |
| Gets eaten a lot | |
| Spotability | 10 |
| Easy to spot | |

SPOTTED

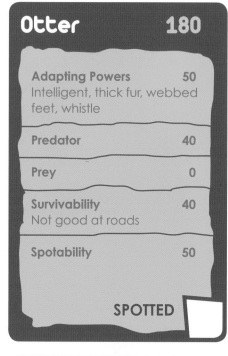

## Otter — 180

| Adapting Powers | 50 |
|---|---|
| Intelligent, thick fur, webbed feet, whistle | |
| Predator | 40 |
| Prey | 0 |
| Survivability | 40 |
| Not good at roads | |
| Spotability | 50 |

SPOTTED

## Kingfisher — 150

| Adapting Powers | 50 |
|---|---|
| Diving Shape, super diver, X-ray eyes | |
| Predator | 50 |
| Prey | -10 |
| Survivability | 30 |
| Not good in flood waters | |
| Spotability | 30 |
| Common but hard to see | |

SPOTTED

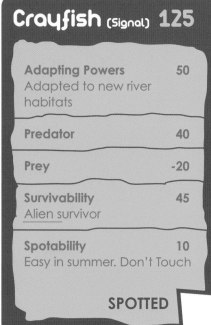

## Crayfish (Signal) — 125

| Adapting Powers | 50 |
|---|---|
| Adapted to new river habitats | |
| Predator | 40 |
| Prey | -20 |
| Survivability | 45 |
| Alien survivor | |
| Spotability | 10 |
| Easy in summer. Don't Touch | |

SPOTTED

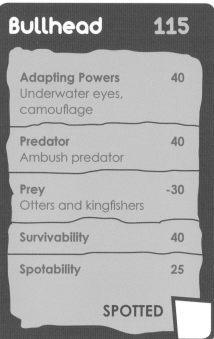

## Bullhead — 115

| Adapting Powers | 40 |
|---|---|
| Underwater eyes, camouflage | |
| Predator | 40 |
| Ambush predator | |
| Prey | -30 |
| Otters and kingfishers | |
| Survivability | 40 |
| Spotability | 25 |

SPOTTED

## Stickleback — 50

| Adapting Powers | 30 |
|---|---|
| Spines, gills | |
| Predator | 20 |
| Small insects, baby fish, eggs | |
| Prey | -25 |
| Survivability | 20 |
| Spotability | 5 |
| Quite easy to find | |

SPOTTED

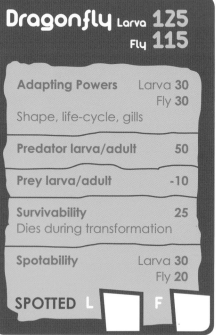

## Dragonfly — Larva 125 / Fly 115

| Adapting Powers | Larva 30 |
|---|---|
| | Fly 30 |
| Shape, life-cycle, gills | |
| Predator larva/adult | 50 |
| Prey larva/adult | -10 |
| Survivability | 25 |
| Dies during transformation | |
| Spotability | Larva 30 |
| | Fly 20 |

SPOTTED L F